Anti-Stress Therapy

Did you have stressful day at work? Are you anxious about your upcoming presentation? Do you want little break from your loud family? Are you nervous about exams? Do you have a creative block? Are you worried about something? Do you need to calm down, 'zone out' and relax without use of medication?

Creative activity, like colouring has many benefits for people of all ages and both genders. Colouring can provide relaxation, meditation, escape from day to day task or worries. During colouring you are focusing on the task at hand and you might forget about your troubles, or in relaxed state, you can come up with a solution to your troubles.

Additionally, colouring can teach you a bit about patience and improves your motor skills. Unlock your creativity and enjoy the benefits of mindful meditation in form of colouring. Find comfortable spot, choose your media and let your mind wander.

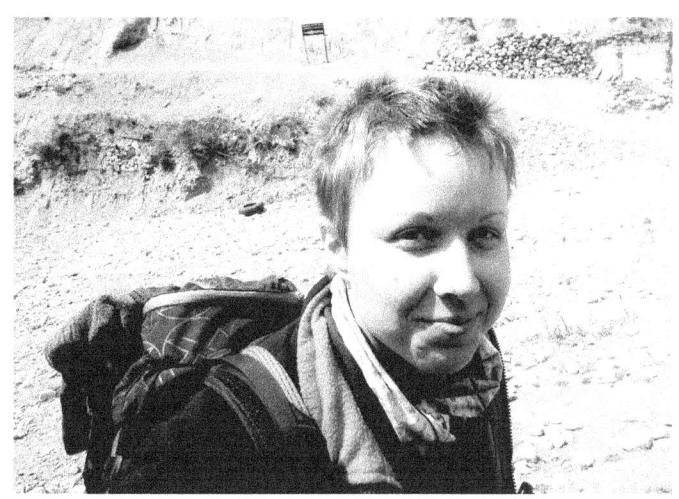

Hana Gregorova

This book is my response to the earthquake that shook in Nepal on 25th of April 2015. I was in Nepal three years ago, this made me aware of the conditions in which the Nepali live and gives me some idea of the consequences the earthquake will have on the country. As one of the poorest countries in the world I realize that the people will need a lot of help to get back on their feet and they will not be able to do it using only their resources, but will need the help of charitable organizations.

My illustrations use a natural and rough style to portray the reality of life in Nepal. Some of the illustrations are simple and some more complex, but through them I would like to appeal to the creativity and playfulness of our inner child. In creating this colouring book I want to move beyond simply raising money; through it, I want to associate life and colour with Nepal, for the country's future.

May 2015

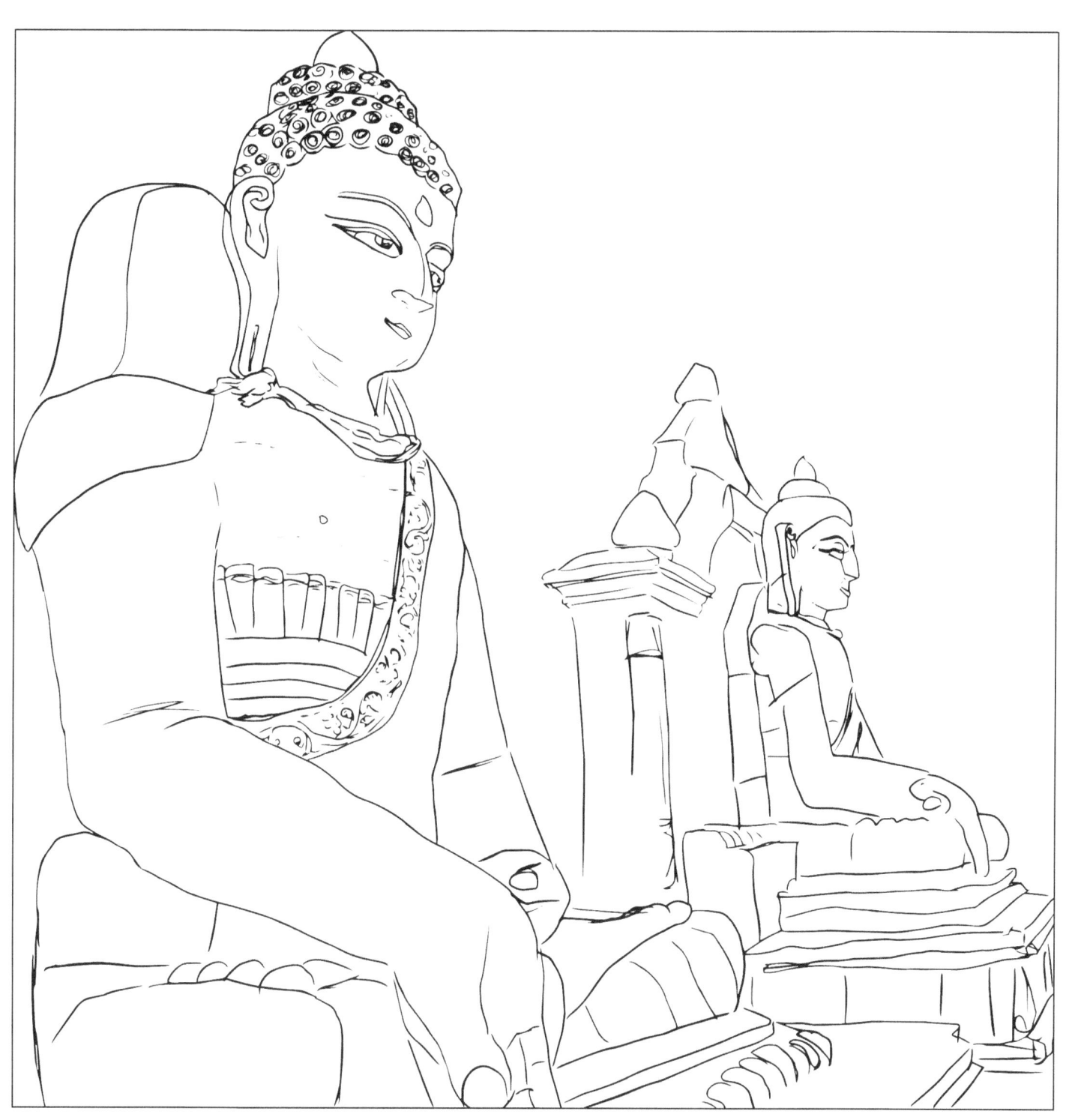

"I am an old man and have known a great many
troubles, but most of them never happened."

Mark Twain

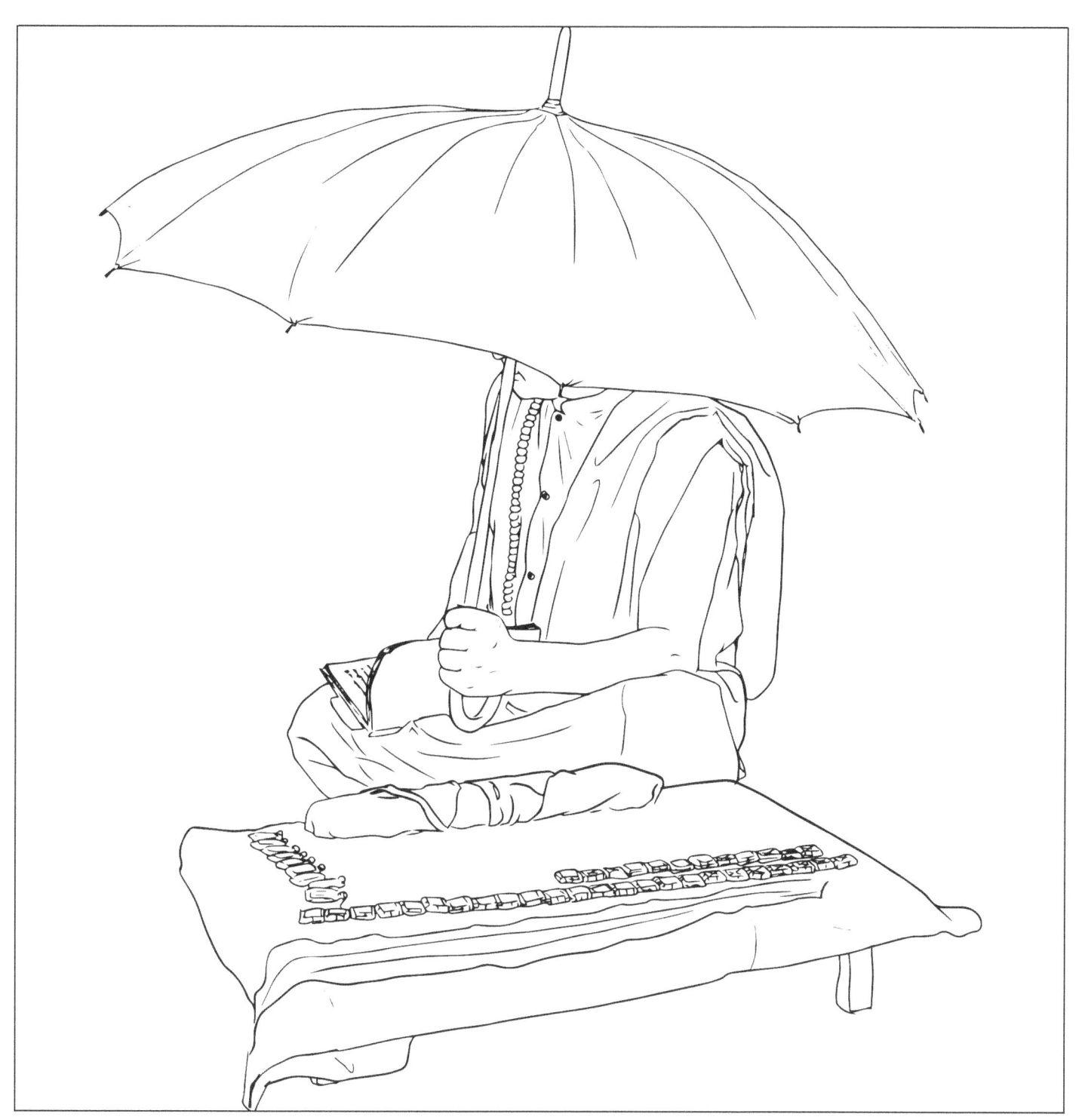

"There is no use worrying about things over which you have no control, and if you have control, you can do something about them instead of worrying."

Stanley C. Allyn

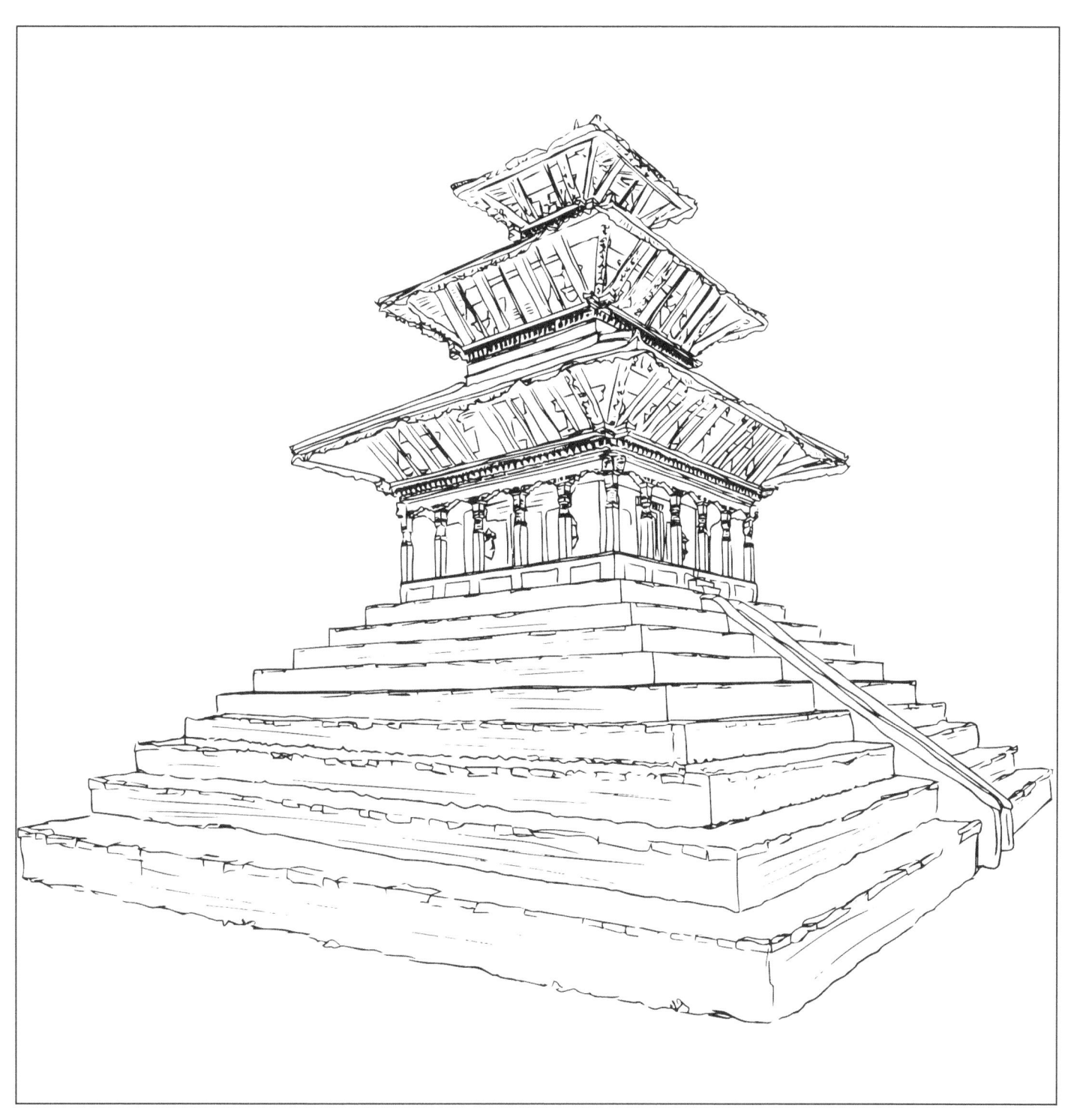

"People become attached to their burdens sometimes
more than the burdens are attached to them."

George Bernard Shaw

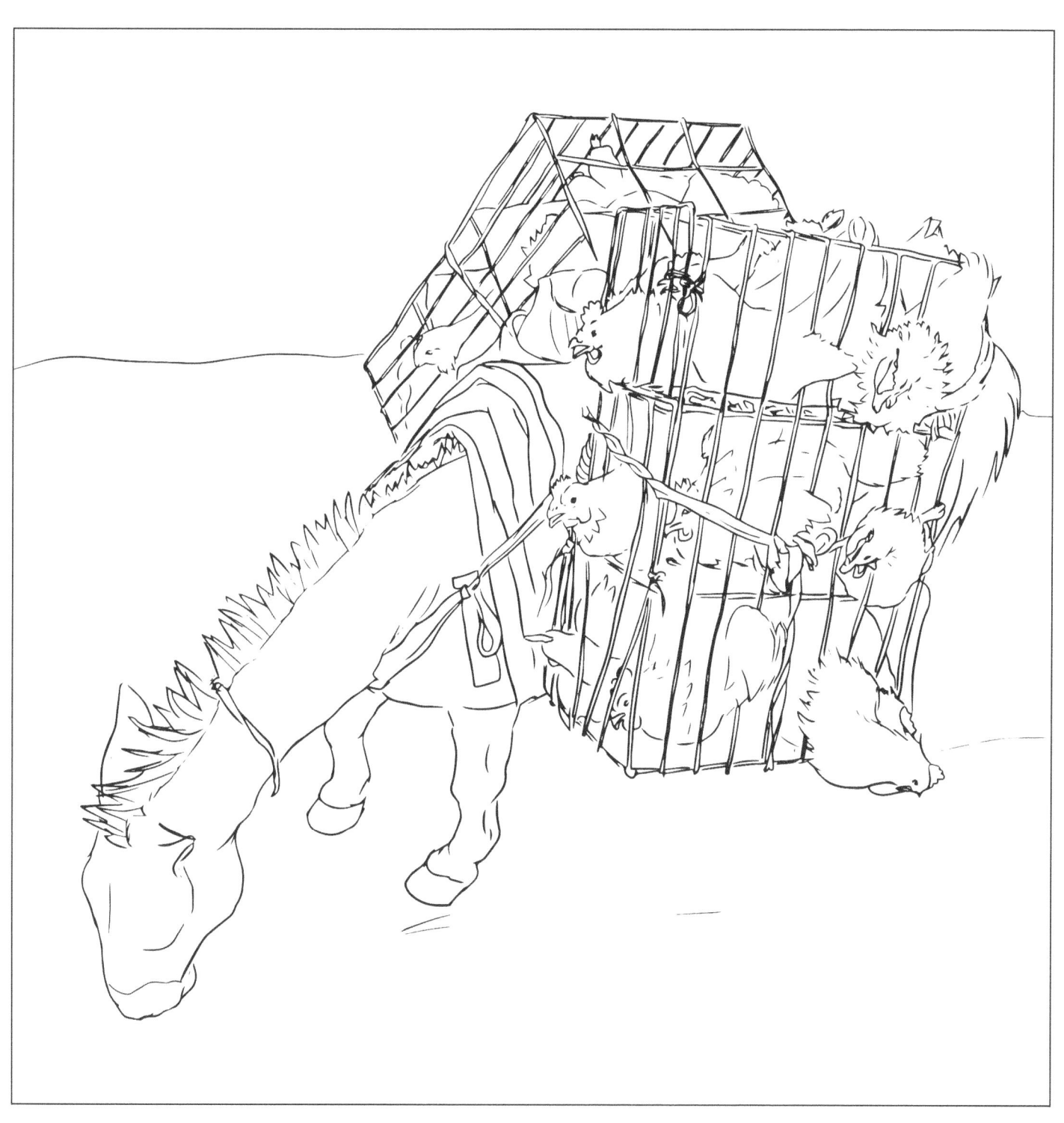

"What happens is not as important as how you react
to what happens."

Thaddeus Golas

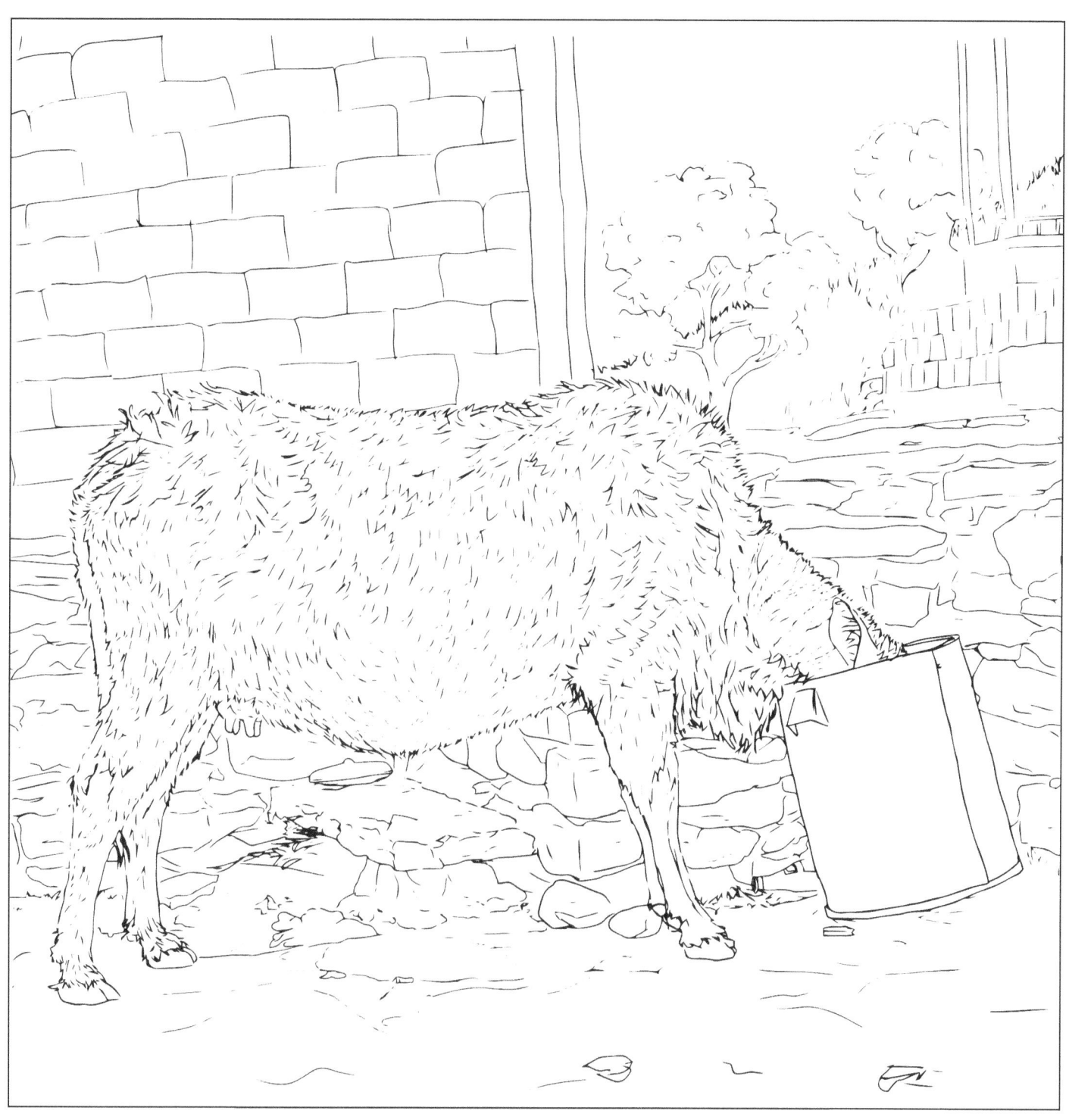

"In times of great stress or adversity, it's always best to keep busy, to plow your anger and your energy into something positive."

Lee Iacocca

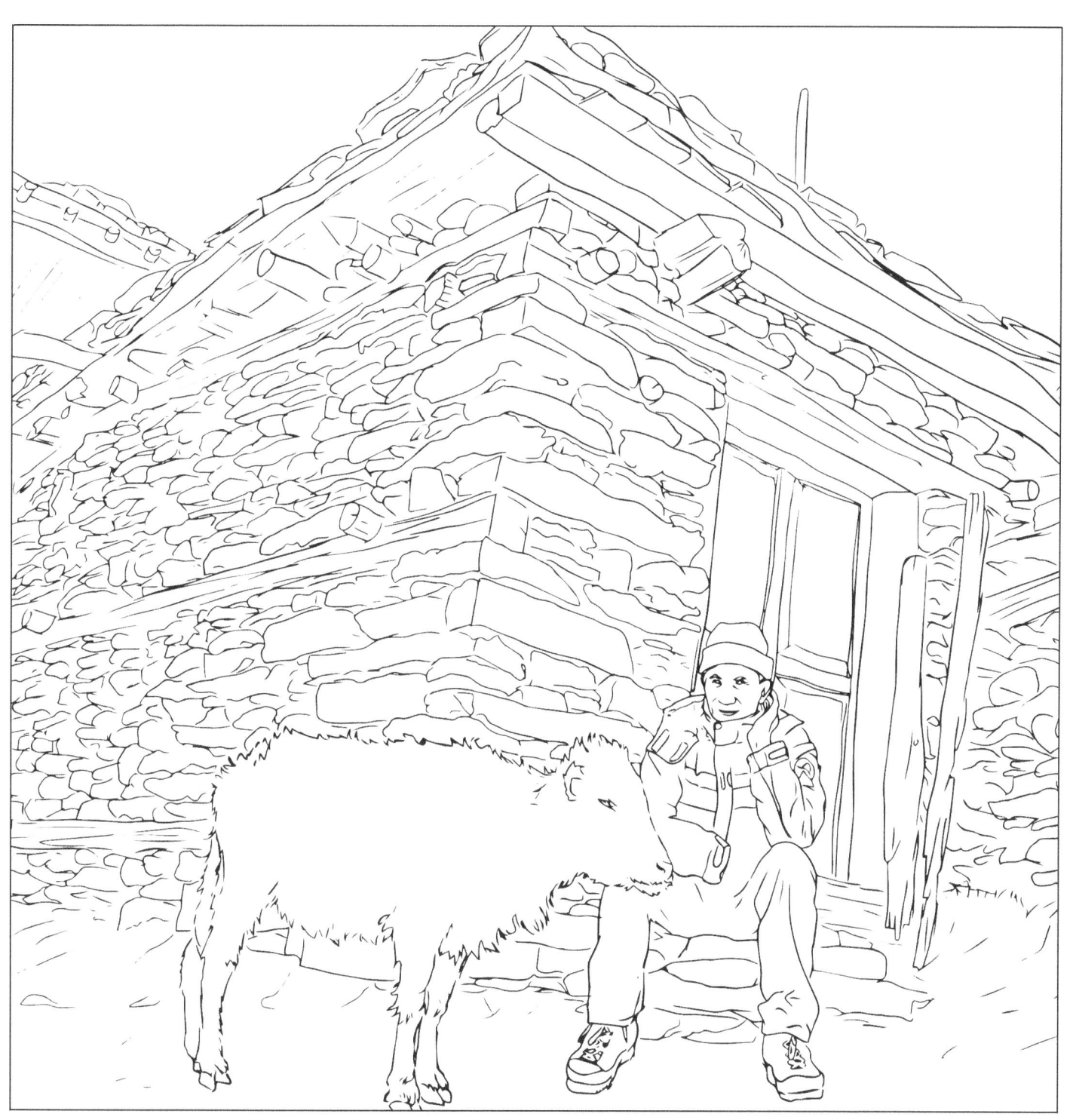

"When you find yourself stressed, ask yourself one question: will this matter in five years from now? If yes, then do something about the situation. If no, then let it go."

Cartherine Pulsifer

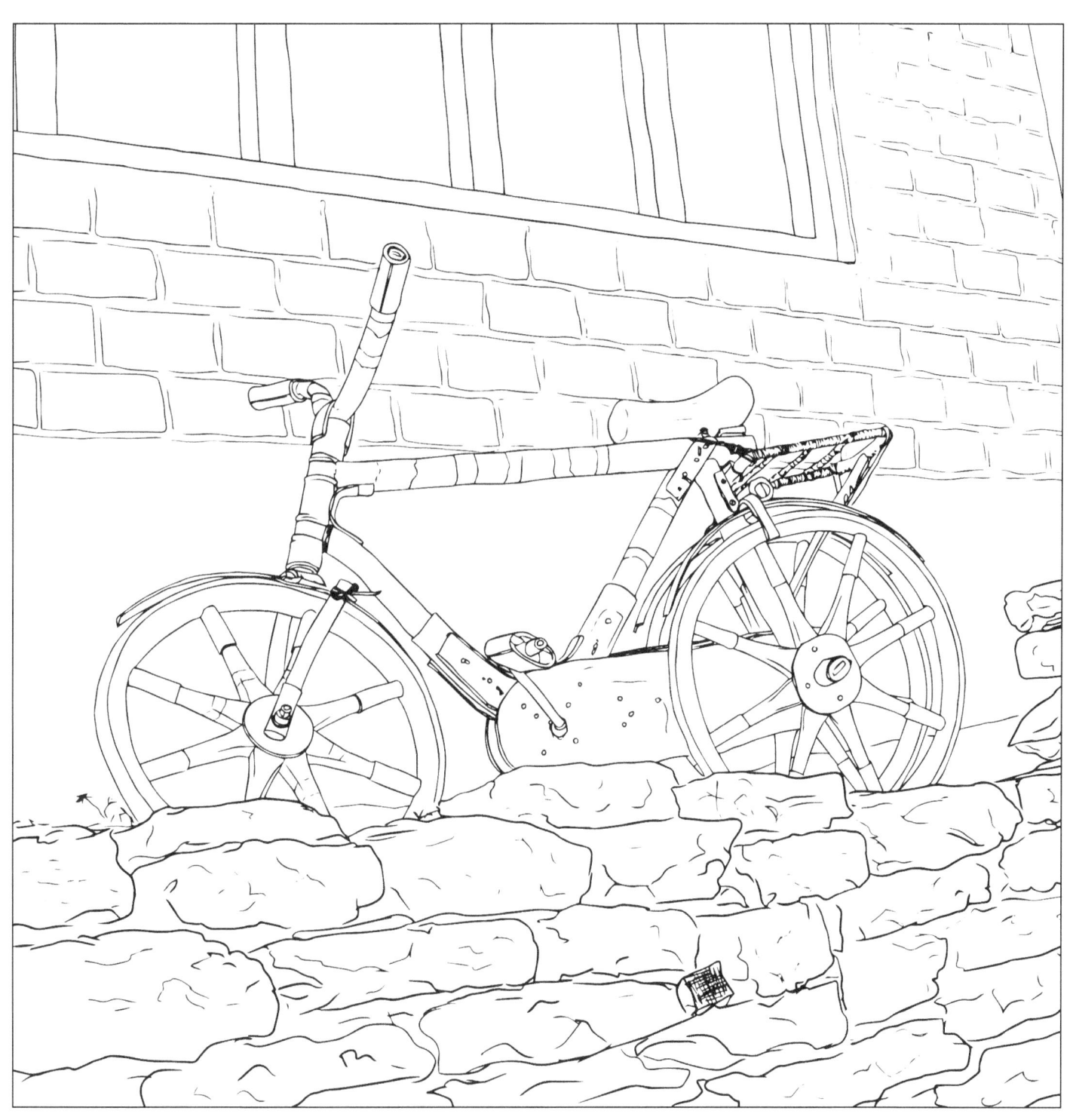

"The more you try to control something, the more it controls you. Free yourself, and let things take their own natural course."

Leon Brown

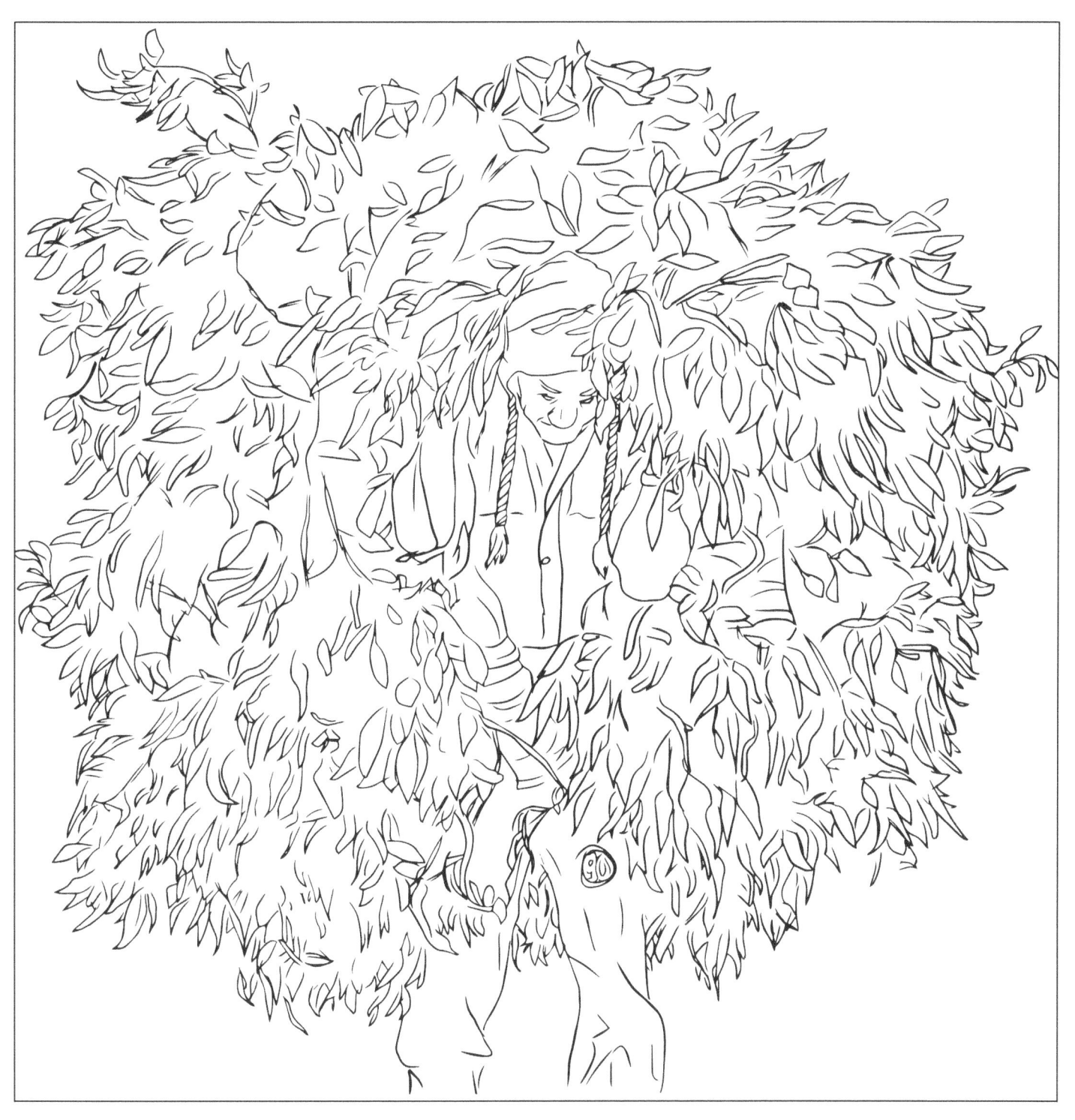

"The time to relax is when you don't have time for it."
~Attributed to both Jim Goodwin and Sydney J. Harris

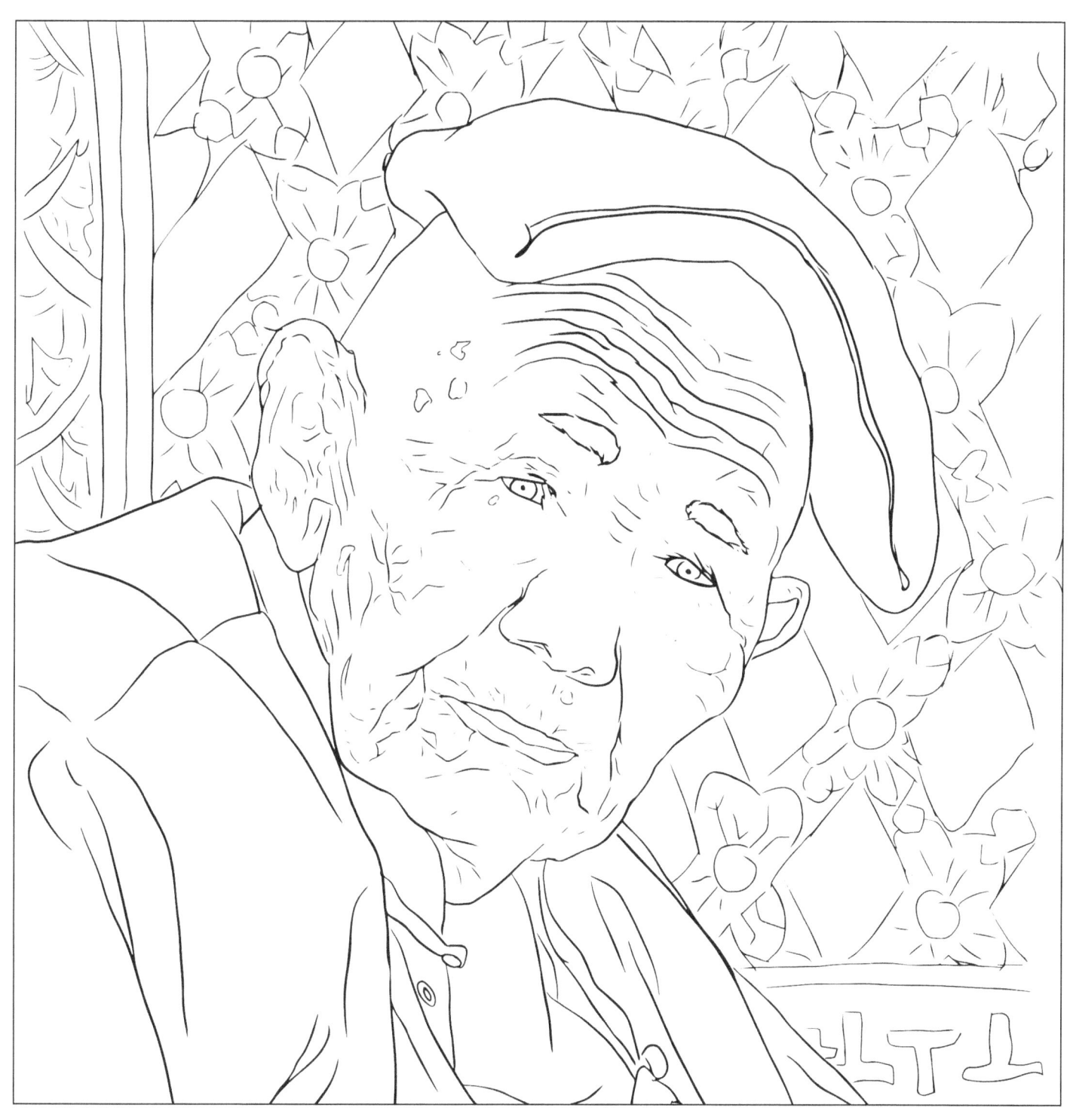

"For fast-acting relief, try slowing down."

Lily Tomlin

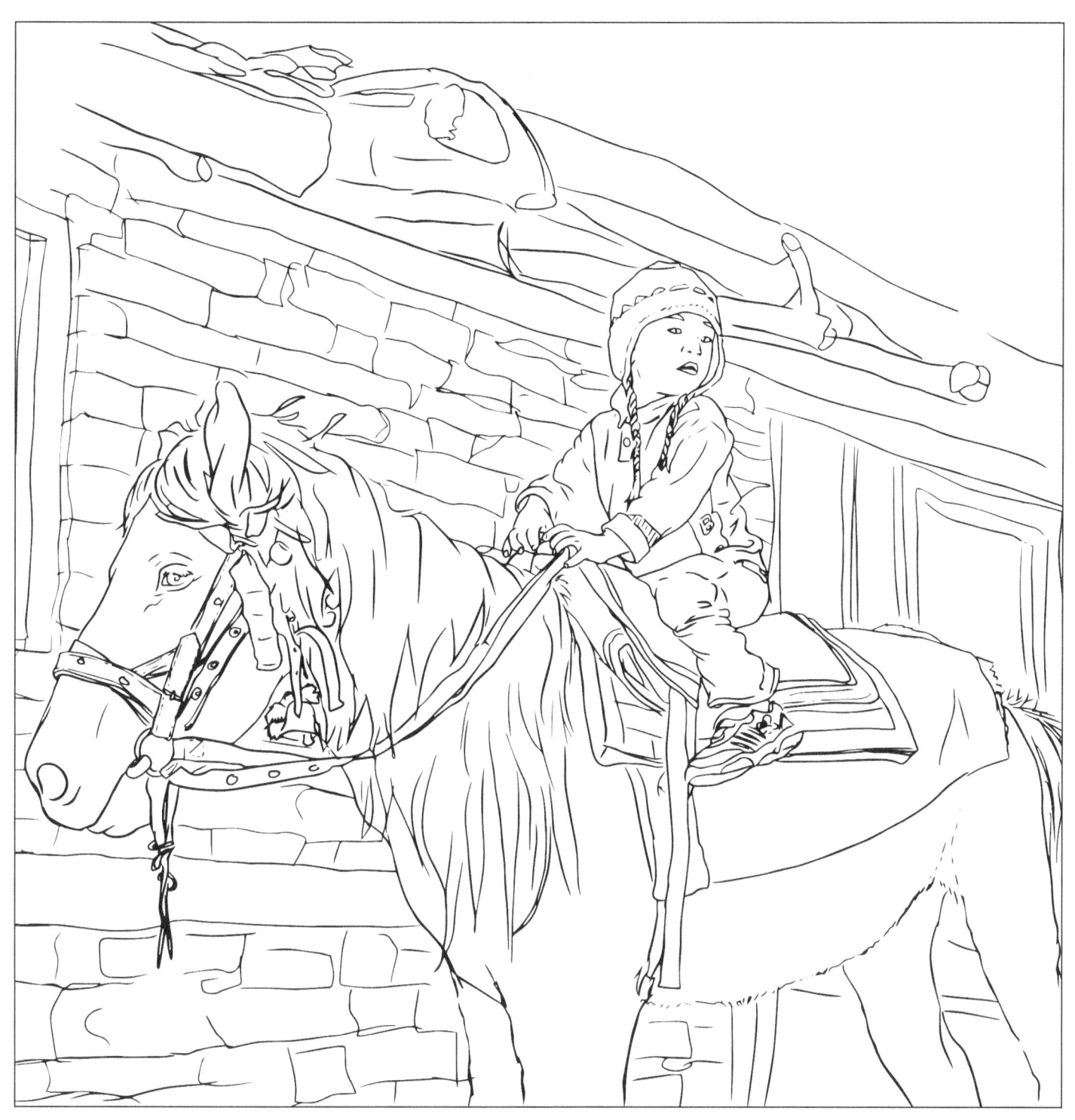

"No one can get inner peace by pouncing on it."

Harry Emerson Fosdick

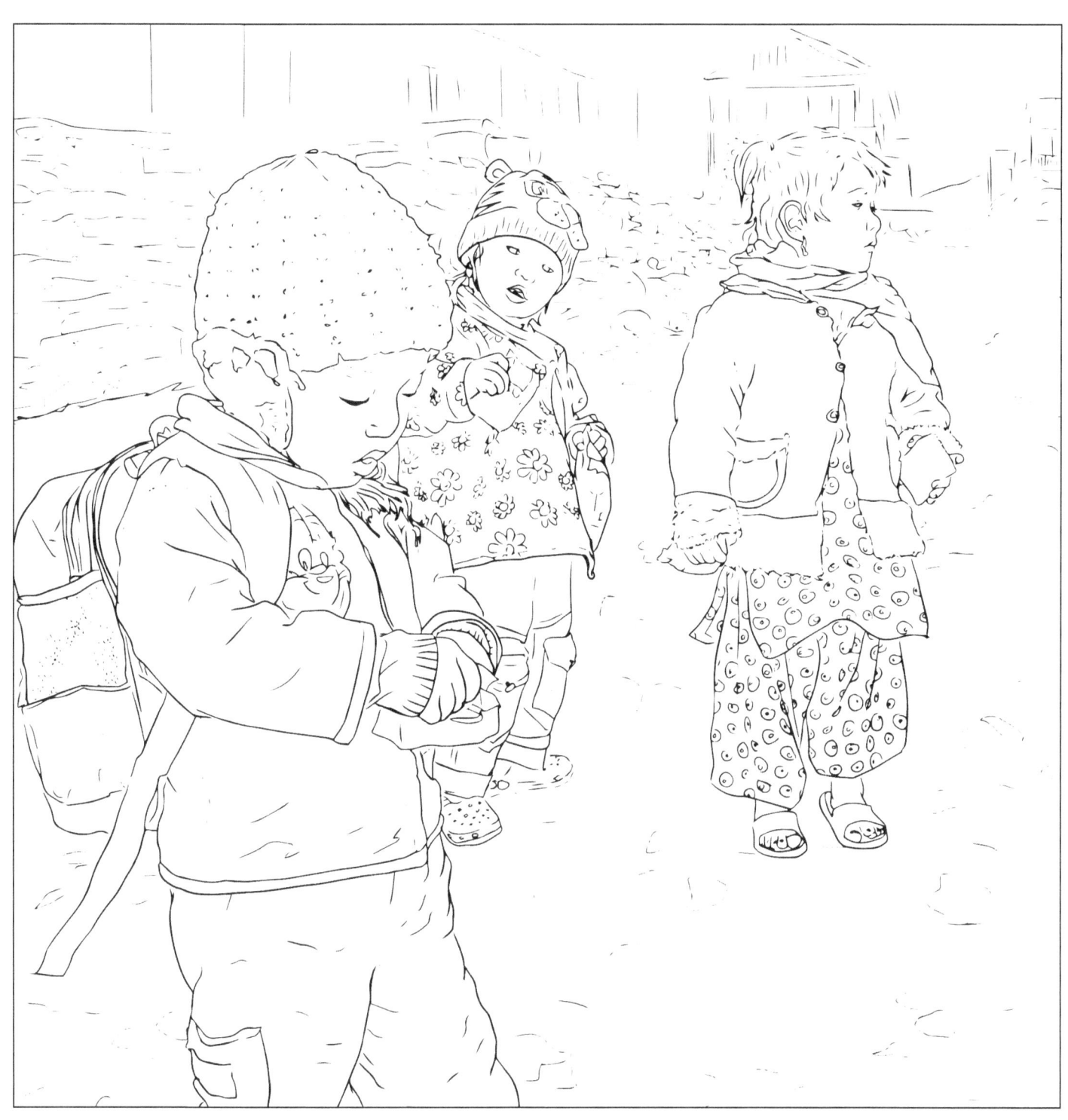

"There is more to life than increasing its speed."

M. Gandhi

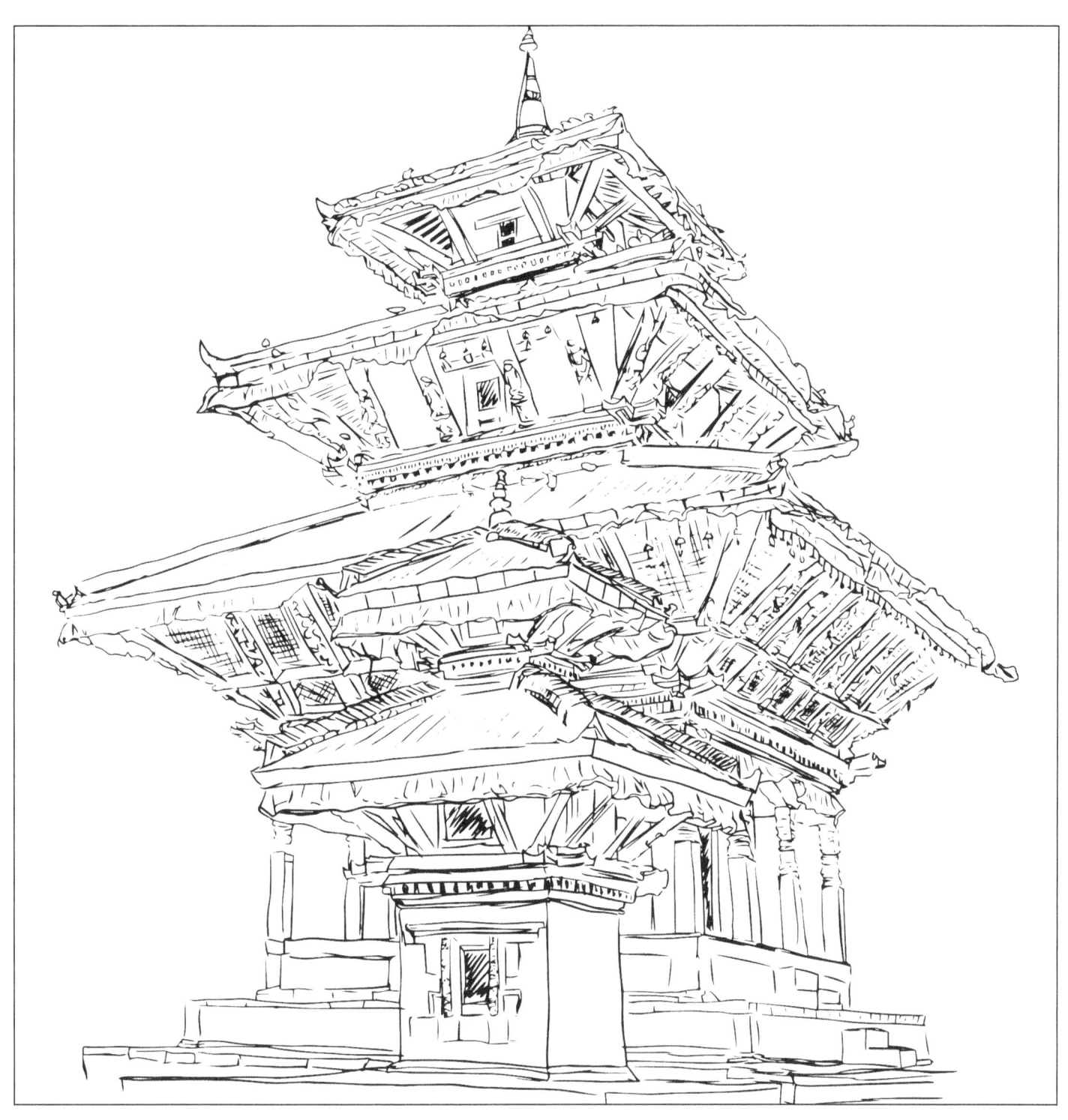

"Our anxiety does not empty tomorrow of its sorrow
but only empties today of its strengths."

Charles H Spurgeon

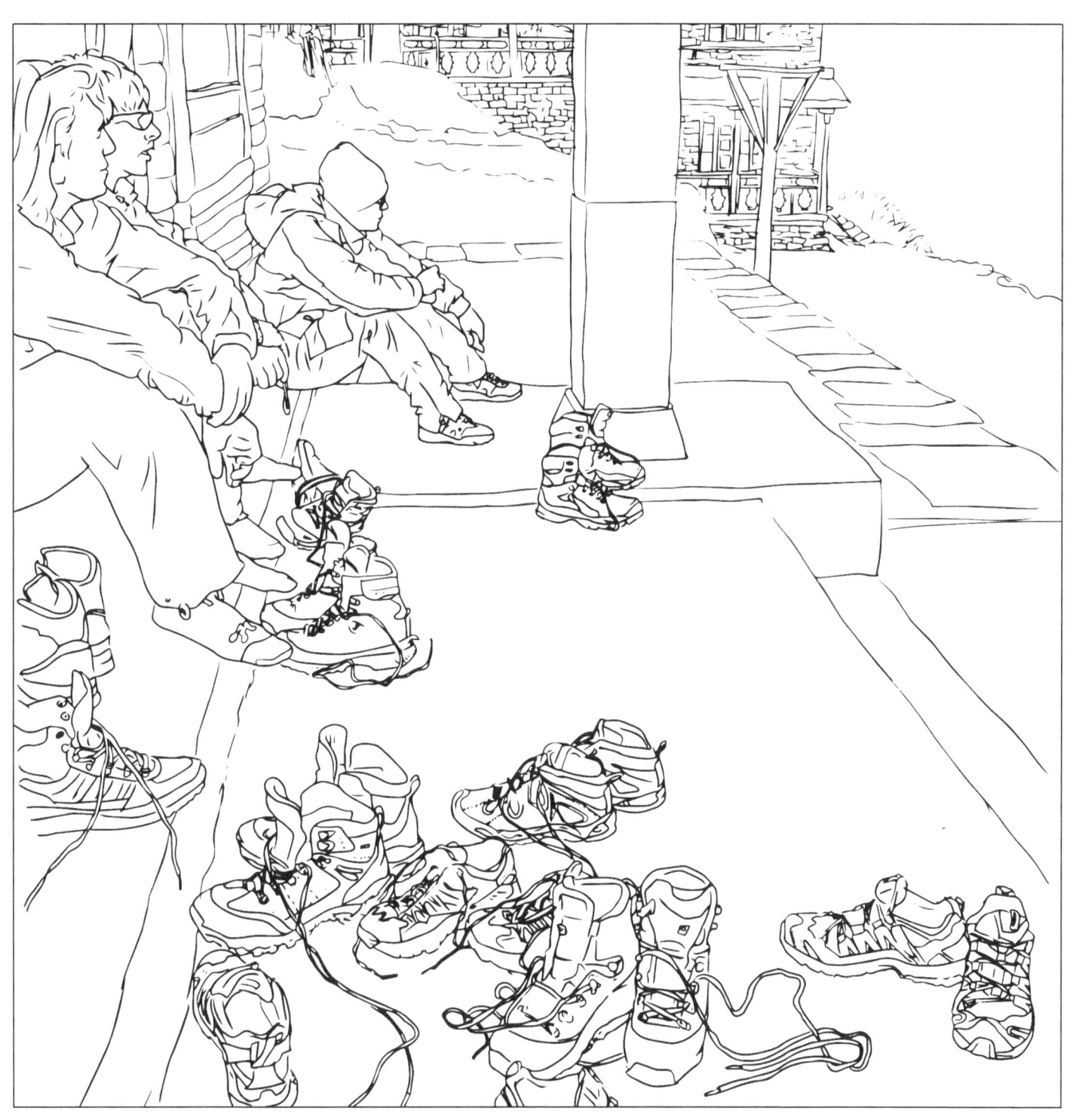

"So often we become so focused on the finish line that
we fail to enjoy the journey."

Dieter F Uchtorf

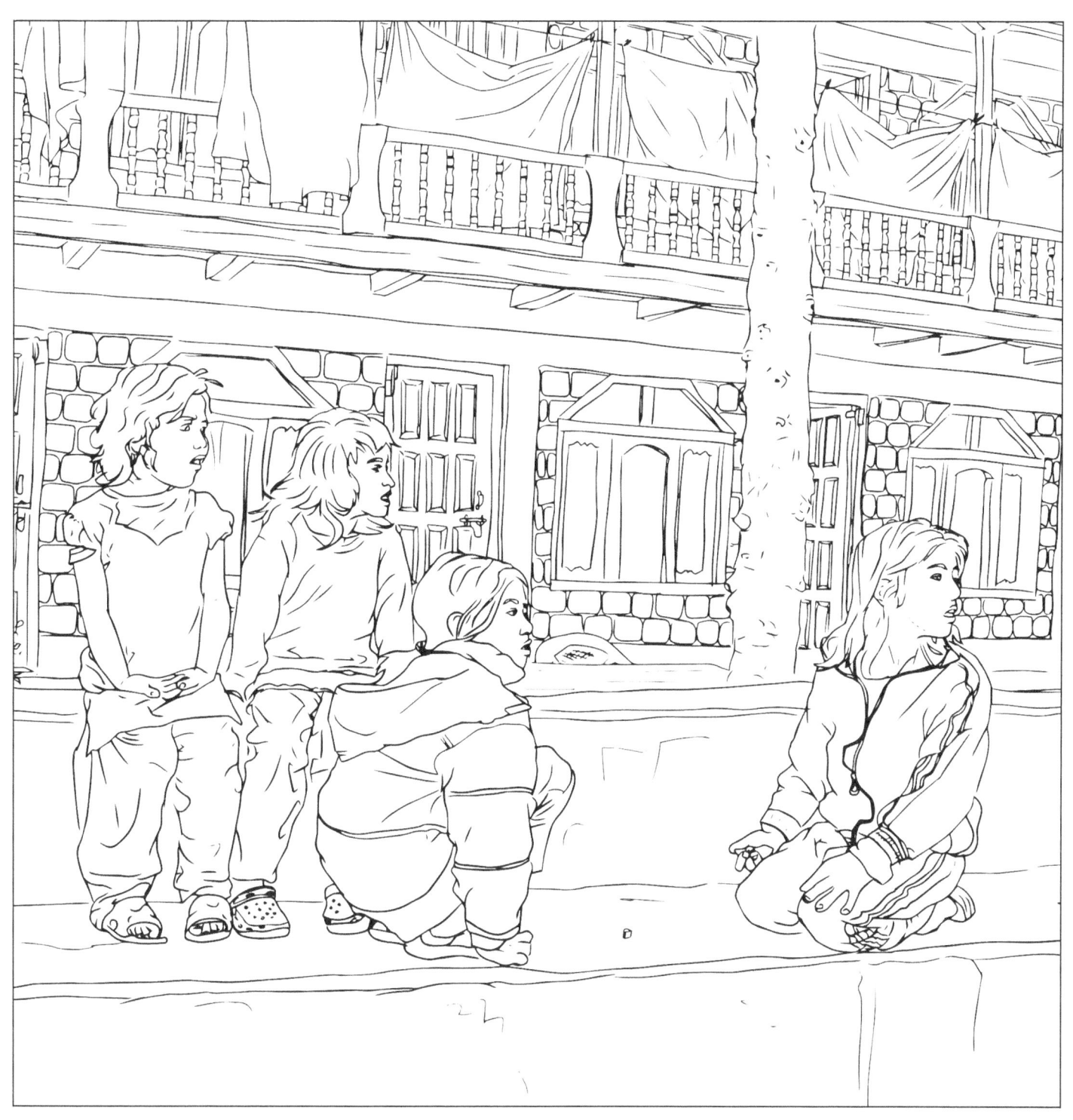

"A day of worry is more exhausting than a week of work."

John Lubbock

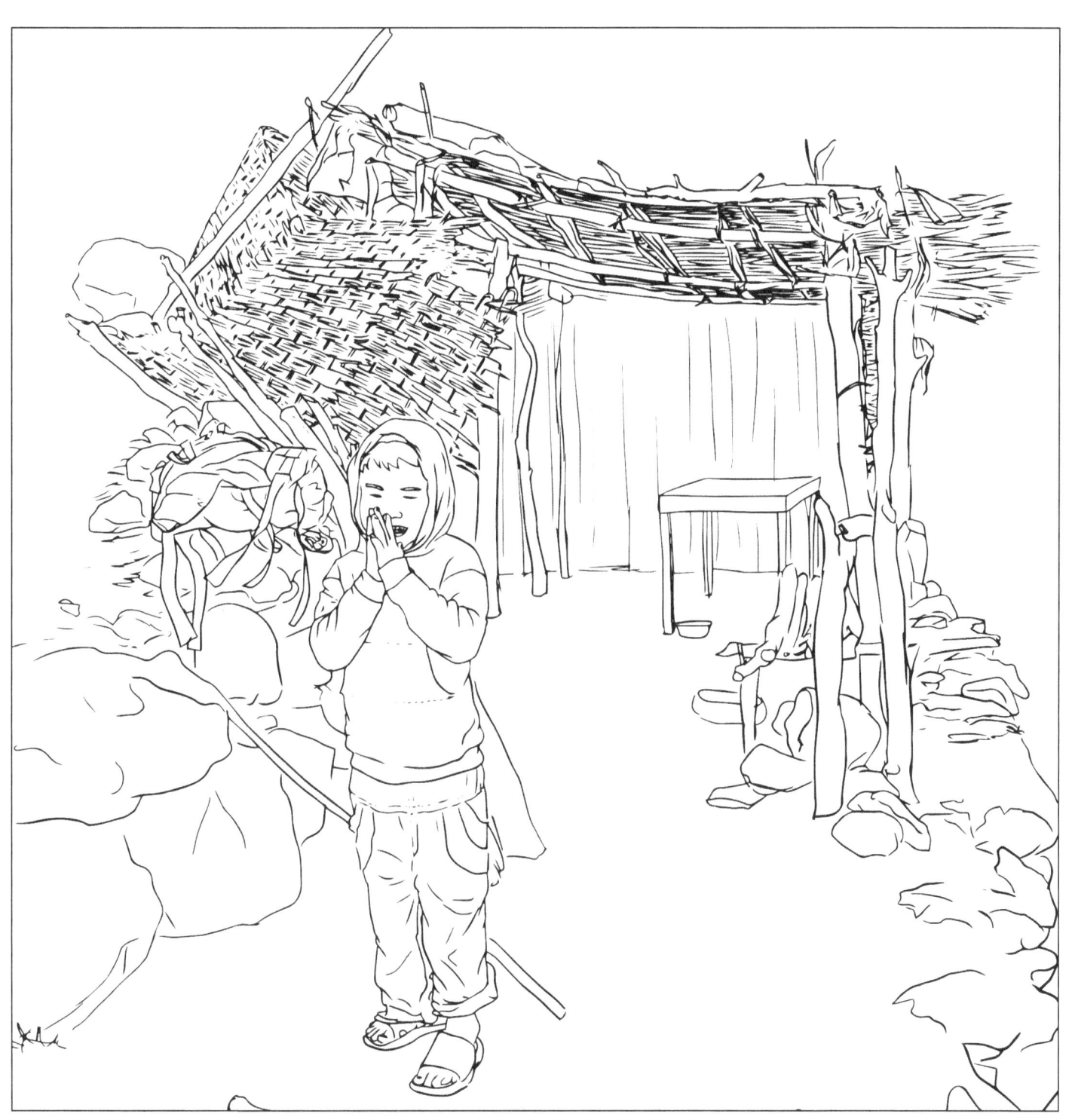

"The greatest mistake you can make in life is to be continually fearing you will make one."

Elbert Hubbard

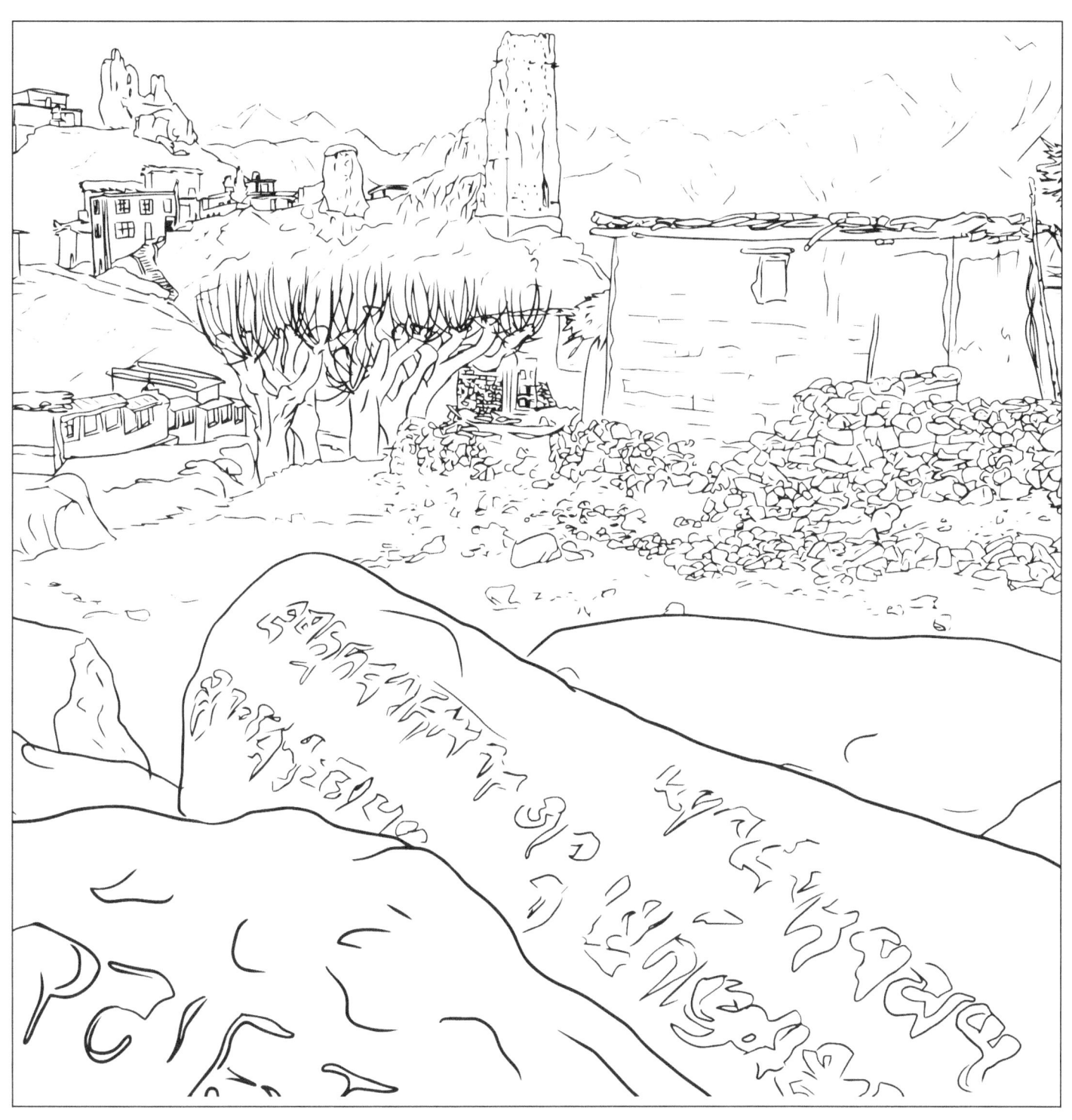

"It is not how much we have, but how much we enjoy
that makes happiness."

Charles Sprugeon

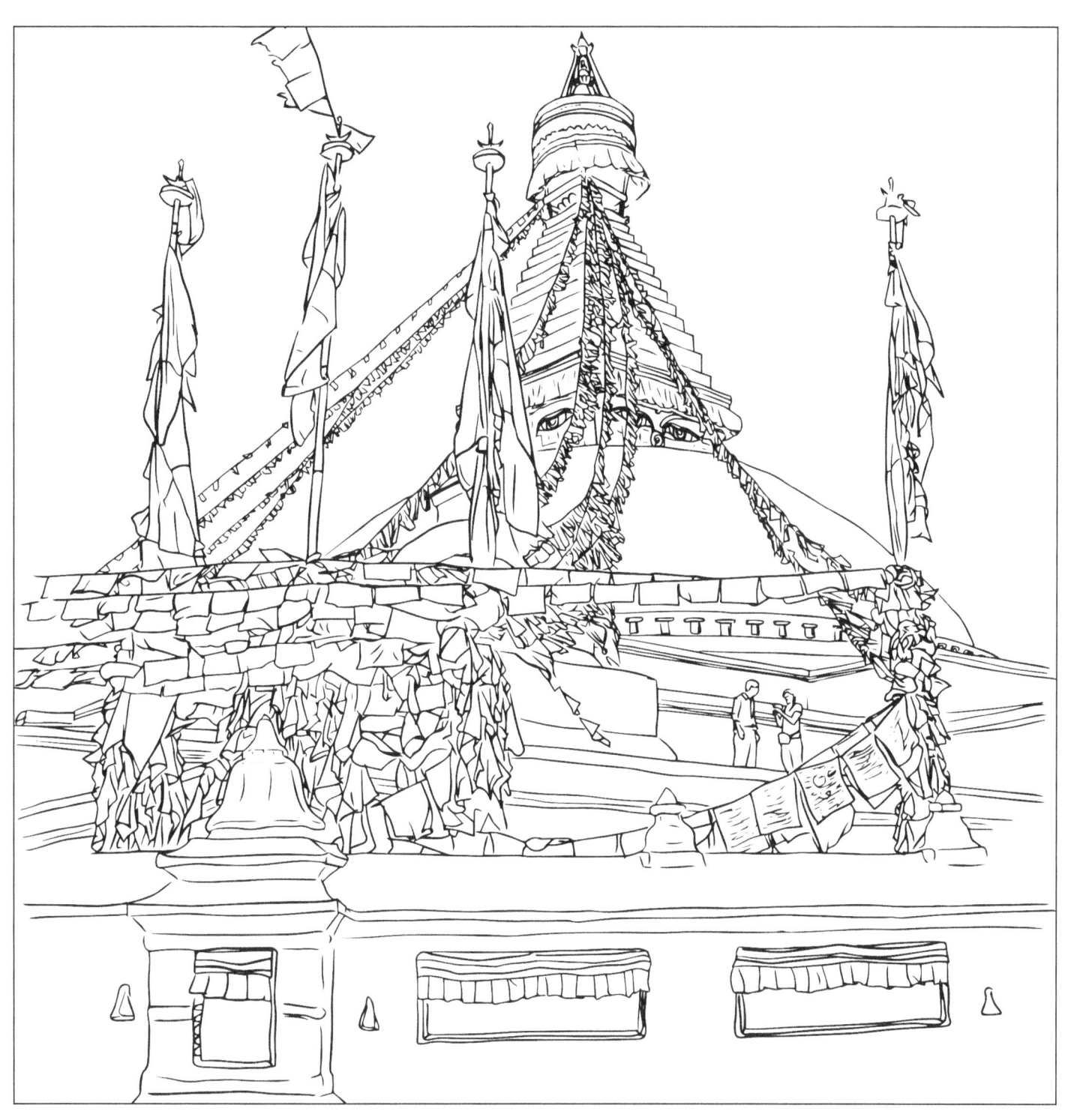

"Stress is like spice – in the right proportion it
enhances the flavor of a dish. Too little produces a
bland, dull meal; too much may choke you."

Donald Tubesing

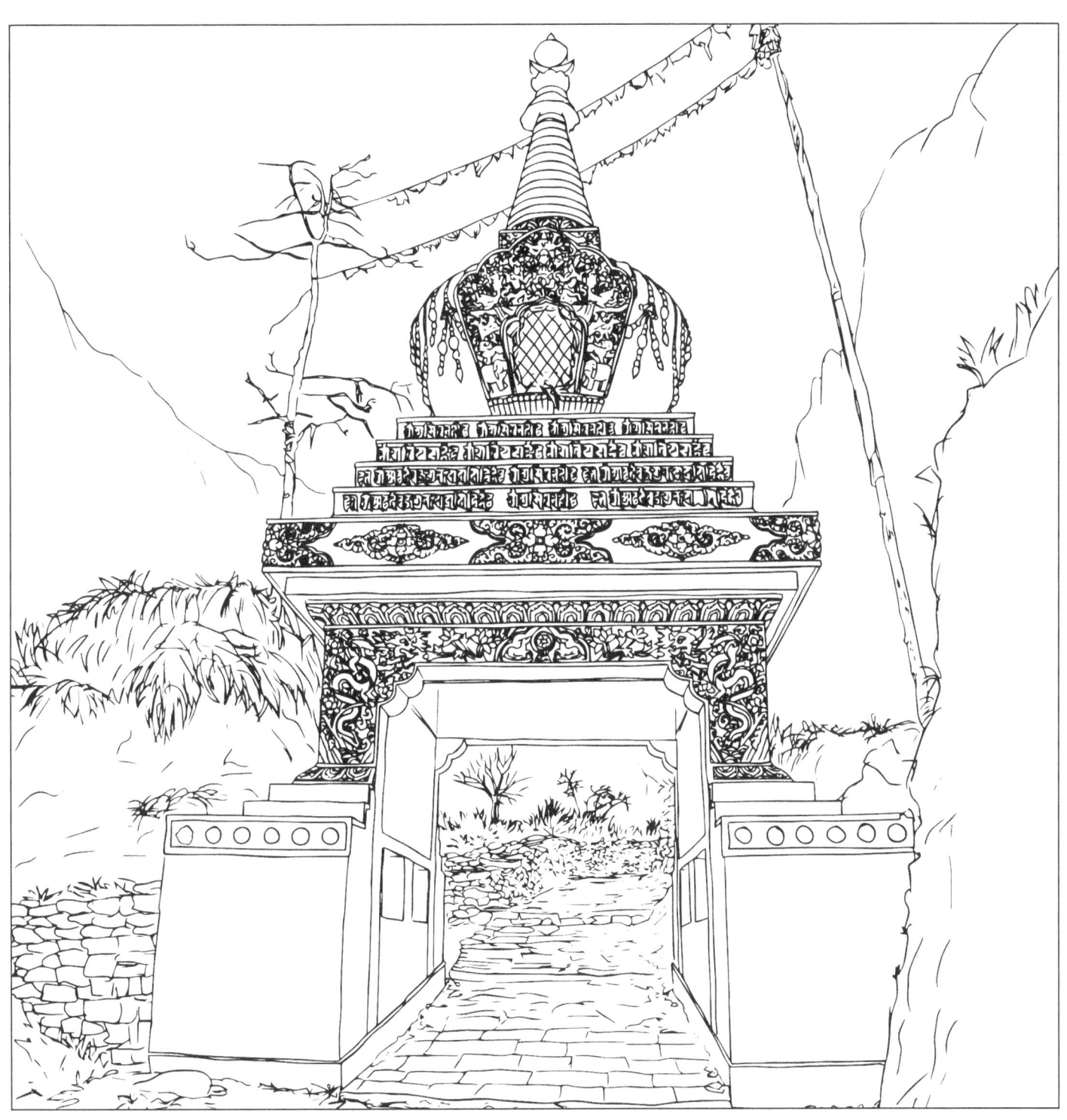

"When we long for life without difficulties, remind us
that oaks grow strong in contrary winds and diamonds
are made under pressure."

Peter Marshall

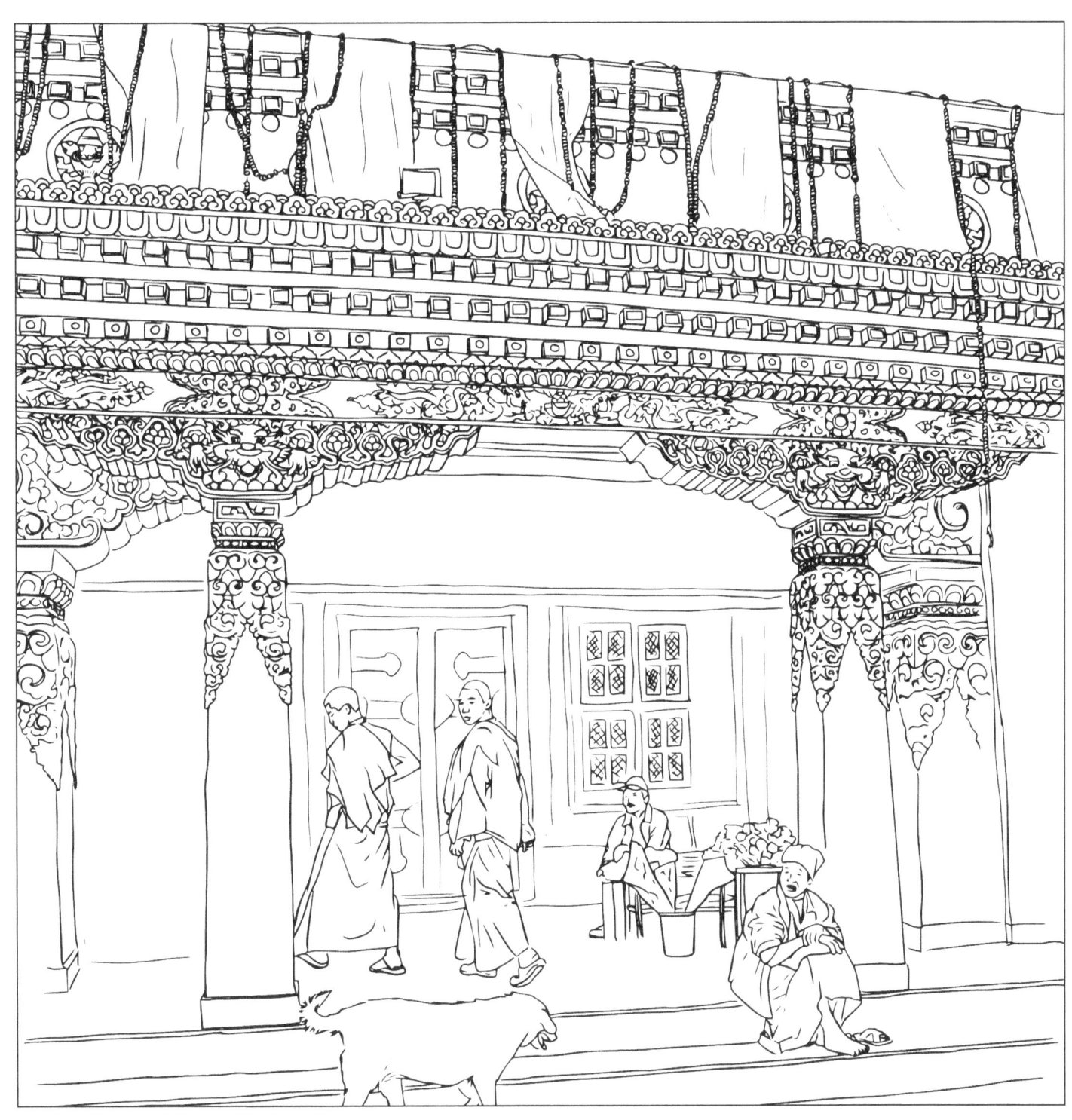

"Life moves pretty fast. If you don't stop and look
once in a while, you could miss it."

Ferris Bueller

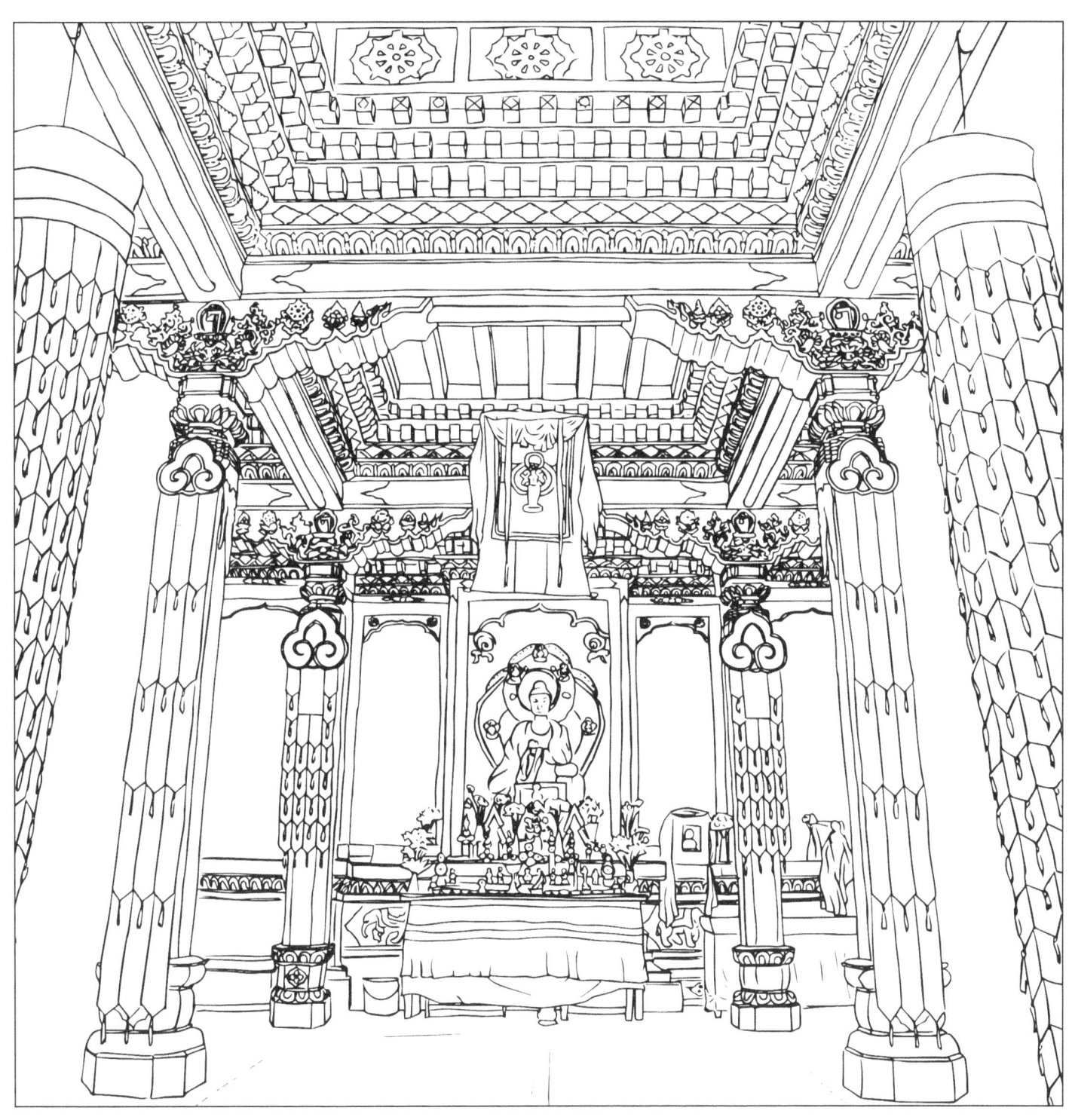

"If we want to live a wholehearted life, we have to be intentional about cultivating rest and play."

Brene Brown

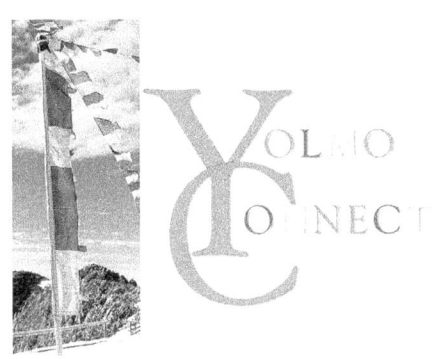

Yolmo Connect

Yolmo Connect is a charity established to support the development of education in the Yolmo Valley in Nepal, particularly, but not exclusively, with regard to IT resources and skills. Corin Hardcastle first visited the remote mountain village of Melamchi Ghyang in late 2012 for six months to work as a volunteer: training teachers and students in computing and IT skills, and helping to equip the school with a computer room and laptops.

Over the subsequent years he continued developing the work at Melamchi and also began to work with other schools in the Yolmo valley, north of Kathmandu. This work was going really well until 25 April 2015 when the earthquake struck.

Corin was himself caught up in the earthquake, working inside the school – all of the children and teachers got out of the school without serious harm, but the school buildings, classrooms and hostels, along with every home in the village, the health centre, and trekkers lodges were devastated. Not one building remained habitable.

Since that time Yolmo Connect has been working to raise funds to rebuild the village and school and to re-establish IT and computer teaching in the area - essential for the future development of education and the communities.

www.yolmoconnect.org

Yolmo Connect partners with other charities, which have links with the school, village and area.

Nepalese Children's Trust: www.nepalesechildrenstrust.co.uk
Community Action Nepal: www.canepal.org.uk
KetaKeti (Belgium): www.ketaketi.be

www.ingramcontent.com/pod-product-compliance
Lightning Source LLC
Chambersburg PA
CBHW080651180526
45168CB00008B/3384